Embracing

Ultimate

Reality

A Soul Path

Brandon Campbell

ISBN: 0-9762135-0-8

First Printing January 2005
Printed in the USA

Editing by Dawn-Louise McLeod
Cover illustration "Majesty" by Laneita Cox
Book design by Fiona Raven

Published by Ascending Realm Publishing
Centennial, Colorado

Ascending Realm Publishing
PO Box 2223
Centennial, Colorado
USA 80161-2223
Email: brandon@ascendingrealm.com
Website: www.ascendingrealm.com

Table of Contents

∽

Acknowledgements

~

Some wonderful people have helped me with this book. And I sincerely appreciate all of the help.

I am grateful to my mother, Judy Campbell, for providing hours of reading, suggestions and comments, and re-reading. I thank my editor, Dawn-Louise McLeod, for all of her wonderful edits and improvements. I also thank Fiona Raven for her graphic assistance and for creating a beautiful presentation for my book.

Finally, I am indebted to those who have supported me as I wrote and rewrote this book: my father, Don Campbell, my sister, Amber Martin, Pete Dubuc, Mike Samuels, Laneita Cox, Winston and Carla Cook, La Nora Potter, Sheila Dorrell and Judy Koucherik.

Prelude

~

      I HAD JUST WON $10 at our church's weekly bingo game. My sister, Amber, said, "If you share half of your winnings with me, then next week, if I win the blackout prize, I'll share half of it with you." The blackout prize was $100, the biggest prize available. However, I wanted to keep all of my money. I visualized riding my bike down to the store to buy $10 worth of candy. Besides, I thought, Amber's not going to win.

My father also coaxed me to share my winnings. But I stood my ground. I went ahead and spent all the money on myself.

The following week, Amber won the blackout prize. I was quiet as we drove home from bingo that evening.

This experience taught me, early in life, a lesson about sharing. Twenty-six years later, I would like to share some of what I have learned along the way.

Embracing Ultimate Reality pays homage to our spiritual essence. It glorifies the higher power that we are all part of.

Enjoy my story while keeping in mind that it could just as easily be yours.

Introduction

∿

ABOUT TWO YEARS AGO, I felt that I needed to write a spiritual book. With much effort, I finally fashioned this book. The chapter entitled "Nighttime Prophecy" helps to explain why this was important to me.

For the last couple of years, I've wanted to share my spirituality with others. Nearly a year ago, I thought I was finished writing this book. My first version was rather "preachy" and very much "out there." The dozen or so people that read that version said positive things, but a few of them told me it would be better if I rewrote it. For the rewrite, I got more personal and tried to qualify much of the mystical aspect with "I believe" or "to me."

I definitely do not want any part of my book to tell people "how it is." I tried that and it did not work: nobody likes being lectured to or preached at. I finally realized how subjective personal spirituality really is. In any case, no person on this planet can really know all the answers to what we are doing here on earth—though some do claim to have that knowledge.

I know this book is still somewhat out there. But I want to keep it that way, because I believe that the true essence of the human spirit is much more than what we see in life. I call this true essence "Ultimate Reality," regardless of whether it exists inside or outside of the spirit. I guess I'm saying that there is more to us all than just what we know in our everyday life. This book is simply about my beliefs and my experiences. My purpose is to share this with others with the hope it can prove valuable in some way to them. I hope, also, that my sincerity and my willingness to share my life will encourage others to do likewise and find their ways spiritually.

Part 1

≈

My Early Journey

CHAPTER I

∾

My Early Illness

MY MOST POWERFUL and earliest memory is of an illness I had when I was four. I remember spending a lot of time in contemplation. Before I describe the illness that this chapter is really about, however, I offer two other incidents from my early life that help to explain my thoughts while I was ill.

When I was three, my mother, Amber, and I went to church one Sunday morning. Amber and I had been baptized as Catholics after my mother had chosen to adopt Catholicism. Up until that time, my mother had not adopted a religion. My father, on the other hand, had had a rural Christian upbringing.

My father was resisting adopting Catholicism and didn't join us on this particular day, although, within a few years, he would attend Catholic church as faithfully as the rest of the family.

Anyway, on this particular Sunday, my father gave me a dime to put in the offering basket at church. I dropped the coin in the basket when it was passed to us.

But I had a specific idea about where the offering basket had come from. When we arrived home, my father asked me about church. I said, "That man, God, brought a basket to church and I gave him my dime." For some reason, both my mother and father were pleasantly surprised to hear me say that.

Around this time, I often played with Amber in our backyard. She is only 17 months older than me, so we usually had fun together.

One day, we came across a large grasshopper. We lived in Tulsa, Oklahoma, where grasshoppers get pretty big.

Amber was about to step on the grasshopper. I said, "Don't kill it." She said, "It's just a bug." I said, "Amber, I care even about a grasshopper." As young as I was, I understood the value of life.

∾

Back to the subject of my illness. When I was four years old, we moved to Stillwater, Oklahoma. Soon afterwards, I began to get very sick. And one of the symptoms was bloody urine. After a trip to our family doctor, I was diagnosed with glomerular nephritis, a kidney disorder. My kidney condition was also accompanied by a severe fever. This ailment turned out to be rheumatic fever.

I remember my parents making a place for me to rest on the couch in the living room. Bed rest is essential with a rheumatic disease and helps to prevent future damage to the vital organs. The couch was one of those that had a pullout bed in it. During the daytime, I was always in plain view and close to either my mother or my father. I remained there each day throughout the two months I was ill. At night, I went to my bedroom to sleep.

During the time I spent in the living room, I slept little. I could not go outside and play. Being sick was quite boring. So my waking moments were filled with thoughts and daydreams, as this was all I was allowed to do.

For the first time in my short life, I began to analyze things. I formulated questions in my mind like: "Why are there so many people in the world?" and "What are all these people doing that's so important?" Although I spent a lot of time with more philosophical thoughts like these, I would also look at a trash company's advertisement in the phone book, see a picture of a garbage truck, and think, "That is what I want to do when I grow up."

I thought about the little I had learned so far about the Catholic religion and the words spoken to me from the Bible. I believed that praying to God would make me get well. So I prayed a lot.

But mostly, I tried to figure out why I was sick. I couldn't understand why I had to lie on a couch all day and just look at the ceiling. I daydreamed, not for fun, but to pass the time. Sometimes, daydreams are not voluntary. Mine were no exception.

My daydreams were filled with people I did not know. These people were usually engaged in some weird conversation or situation that I did not understand. It seemed like every other day I envisioned someone lecturing to me as I lay in that couch.

Now I believe that what at the time I thought were daydreams might actually have been astral experiences. Maybe all of my visions of strange conversations had been real, just not real to our material world.

I also believe that my spirit was trying to decide whether or not to abort my life. I believe my spirit knew that, if I stayed here, I would face significant physical challenges in my future.

It's a cliché, but I believe that everything happens for a reason. Whether this illness had a significant influence on who I am today, it played a role in preparing me for life. In the months I spent on that couch, I learned what can sometimes take many months, years, even a lifetime, to learn.

~

CHAPTER 2

Another Serious Illness
and Miraculous Recovery

IN 1978, SHORTLY AFTER ENTERING the second grade, I contracted another illness even more severe than glomerular nephritis and rheumatic fever, and I had to go to the hospital—two hospitals, as it turned out.

The night before I became ill, my mother had a dream, or vision—a warning—to watch over me as I slept. Although she didn't know exactly what it meant, she mentioned it to my father.

Fortunately, my parents acted on that dream. Before I went to sleep that night, they made a bed for me in the living room. They moved in the mattress from my bedroom and then put down blankets and pillows. I was excited about sleeping there. I loved having a pallet to sleep on.

My mother slept in the living room that night, while

my father slept in their bedroom. Perhaps my mother was a little more concerned about me since she had had such a vivid vision earlier.

I awoke around midnight and tried to get up for a glass of water. But I had a severe headache and could barely walk.

Hearing my efforts, my mother awoke almost immediately. Within a couple of minutes my father, too, was awake. My mother called the doctor. She was so frightened that she could hardly dial the phone (touchtone phones didn't yet exist).

As it was the middle of the night, my mother had to leave a message for the doctor. But she was so scared that she forgot to leave him our number. Since the doctor was not at his office, he didn't have the number to return her call. About 15 minutes later, my mother phoned the doctor again and left the correct number. A few minutes later, our doctor returned the call and said he would coordinate with the local hospital about me. When our doctor finally notified the hospital and called my parents back, we immediately drove to the hospital. About 45 minutes had elapsed from the time I woke up to the time we arrived at the emergency room of the local hospital in Stillwater.

Soon after we arrived there, the doctors told my parents that the hospital was not capable of dealing with the severity of my illness. The doctors knew that a small hospital used to serving a population of 20,000 could not fully help me. So they told my parents to take me 50 miles to the Children's Hospital in Oklahoma City and notified Emergency there.

I still remember the drive—I was wrapped in a blanket, but could not get to sleep until we were almost there.

When I awoke, it was the next morning, and I was in the emergency room at Children's. I still had a severe headache. I also was naked. I did not like that at all. My mother was quite firm with the nurse about getting me a gown. Eventually, the nurse gave me one, but, much to my discomfort, it was completely open at the back. I felt as if she were thinking something like, "Big deal—he's just a kid, so who cares if he's naked." By the end of the day, I had been relocated to an isolation room. I was diagnosed with meningitis; specifically, meningeal encephalitis. This condition came with a constant headache due to the abnormal amount of water on my brain.

The doctors kept me in the isolation room for five days. During this time, I had to endure a couple of spinal taps. The first one was excruciating. A couple of days later when one of the hospital neurologists told me I had to have another one, I felt my heart sink—I knew the pain I was in for. Sure enough, the second one wasn't much better.

The CAT (Computerized axial tomography) scan procedures were just as bad as the spinal taps, although the scan itself was okay. For that, I simply lay on a table that moved through a big tunnel where instruments performed the scan. It was what happened prior to each scan that was bad. Each time, I had to get a shot of dye in my ankle. The needle looked as if it were several inches long. That particular shot was about three times as painful as any other I had experienced. All in all, I had five CAT scans.

After five days in isolation, I was moved to a room with other children, on one of the main floors of the hospital. The bed was less comfortable, but, unlike the isolation room, the new room had a window. The bit of excitement I had from moving to the new room disappeared the next day, however, when another hospital doctor came in. He said that I had to have a third spinal tap. This was supposed to be the final one.

Immediately after that procedure, Amber handed me a little stuffed animal she had purchased from the hospital gift shop. It was a dark brown puppy. I have always had a propensity for naming my possessions, my pets, and, as I later explain, my spiritual guides. I was in so much pain that the only name I could think of for this puppy was "Darky." I guess that, after that last spinal tap, I was not up to the task of finding a more original name for my toy.

During my illness, many people prayed for me, because they knew that this illness could kill me. I vaguely remember the priests, preachers, pastors, and ministers from different religious denominations that came, at my parents' request, to pray for me. People back in Stillwater including those in both my Sunday school and elementary school classes prayed for me, too.

After ten days in Children's, I remember looking up at the door jam in my room. For a second, I saw Jesus smiling at me. I knew it was Him, because His face was similar to pictures of Him I had seen. Immediately after His image disappeared, I knew that I would recover from my illness.

I turned to my parents, who were in the room with me, and told them what I had just seen. I felt an overwhelming sense of peace. I was not worried about my illness anymore. I told my parents my illness would go away and I would be fine. This sense of "knowing" has never left me.

By now, the doctors were telling my parents how badly off I was. According to my previous CAT scan, the water on my brain was not diminishing. The doctors were adamant about taking the next step.

This was to put a shunt, a type of bypass tube, between my brain and my heart to drain the water from my brain. First, however, I had to be subjected to yet another scan to determine how much water was still on my brain. This scan happened the day after I had seen the face of Jesus.

After the scan, the doctors went in a room to view the results. These results perplexed the doctors. The abnormal amounts of water were gone. The doctors were not able to explain it. My parents told the doctors that it was not explainable, but that it was a blessing.

With the disappearance of the abnormal amount of water, my body began to recover from the meningitis. On the day after my final CAT scan, one of the hospital doctors tested me in order to evaluate my recovery and help determine when I could go home.

The doctor put a straight line of masking tape, about six feet long, on the hall floor. He said that when I could walk on it without losing my balance, I could go home.

I tried hard to walk the line but could not. So the doctor said I would have to stay another week before I could try again.

During that next week, I thought a lot about walking that straight line and convinced myself that I had to walk it at my next chance. After the week had passed, I was given another opportunity with the tape. This time I walked it without losing my balance. The next day, my family and I went home to Stillwater.

∾

CHAPTER 3

Content with God, and the Inky Experience

WITHIN SIX WEEKS, I had fully recovered from my illness. I returned to school and resumed going to church with my family.

My recent experience of seeing Jesus had given me a strong desire to learn more about religion. Over the next couple of years, I read most of the Bible.

My favorite book in the Bible was the Book of Psalms. I even copied some of the verses onto loose-leaf paper and kept them in a folder. I only copied the verses that had meaning to me. Even at the age of eight, I was trying my best to understand God.

As I wrote this chapter, I opened that childhood folder, which my parents had kept for me all these years, and re-read what I had written.

The most striking words refer to Psalm 14:2. Although most versions of the Bible differ slightly from each other, this verse says,

> *"The LORD looked down from*
> *Heaven on the children of men, to see if*
> *there were any who did understand, who did*
> *seek after God."*

∼

My folder contains another treasure. It is a prayer I wrote. I would have been between eight and nine years old when I wrote it. I include it here in its original form, complete with grammatical mistakes:

God the Father

> *God is our Father the almighty maker of*
> *heaven and earth. His son Jesus Crist*
> *Wich has saved us by dieing for our sins.*
> *Taking away our sins for us to live...*
> $\qquad$ *Amen.*

∼

A few months after my recovery, Amber had a birthday. Two days before, my parents had told me we were getting her a female puppy. They said that it was a Cocker Spaniel, but I did not know what that was. They also told me that the puppy already had a name.

I thought, "If the puppy already has a name, then I need to know what it is." So I crawled behind one of the big chairs in the living room and asked God to give me the answer. It came immediately—"Inky."

I thought that Inky was a funny name for a dog. So I convinced myself that this answer could not be right. I continued trying to get the name but soon decided I was wasting my time.

On my sister's birthday, we all went to pick up the puppy. A few Cocker Spaniel puppies greeted us. I noticed that one of them was jet black. The owner picked her up, handed her to my sister, and said, "This is Inky."

God had indeed given me the name of the puppy, just as I had asked. When the owner told me the name of the puppy, I knew I had done something special. But, at the same time, it scared me. It scared me because I did not understand how I knew the name. I did not know then about what is referred to as the "sixth" sense.

I didn't tell anyone about this foresight, other than mentioning it in passing. The only responses I got to any comment I might have let slip was along the lines of, "That's nice," and a look of sheer disbelief.

Unfortunately, instead of learning why this name might have come to me, I let it go. I never wanted to invite an experience like that into my life again, at least not then, because I did not understand it. And I had never heard of anybody encouraging that type of thing, at least not in Oklahoma and certainly not in church.

What is now clear to me was that this "seeing" or premonition-type experience was an opportunity—one which I passed up—for me to learn about my spirit and its divine nature. Because I did not realize what I was giving up, however, I didn't feel bad about it.

≈

CHAPTER 4

From Theist to Atheist

SOON AFTER I ENTERED the fourth grade, I transferred to a Lutheran school in Enid, Oklahoma, along with three of my friends. This was the solution to what my parents, some of my friends and their parents, and I identified as problems with the "quality" of the fourth-grade offering. To us, it seemed that our teacher at the public school didn't care much about our education. Teaching was just a job to Mrs. Warden.

My parents sent me to a Lutheran school, because the only Catholic school in Enid had closed. They told me that the Lutheran religion was very similar to the Catholic religion. I was happy that I would get exposure to another religion, because God and attending church was so important to me.

The school was St. Paul's Lutheran School, which

I attended for two years. It was quite different from the two public schools I had attended before. First, as might be expected, a significant part of the curriculum revolved around religion. Every week, students attended a one-hour church service, or "Chapel," at the community church that was part of St. Paul's.

Second, along with the standard elementary school education, our studies included most of the Lutheran Bible. Curiously, not until my college music education nine years later did I learn about Martin Luther and fully comprehend his works against the Catholic Church.

I remember one assignment in particular. Everyone in the class had to memorize The Ten Commandments and be tested. Back then, it seemed like a lot of work. As I was memorizing the commandments, I thought a lot about what they meant. This was one of the few assignments, throughout my scholastic career, that has had a lasting impact on me. And, by the way, I received an "A" for that assignment.

At the same time that I attended St. Paul's, I went almost weekly to St. Francis Catholic Church with my family.

When I was about 12, the priests at St. Francis asked me to be an altar boy. I gladly accepted the honor.

A couple of months later, Amber decided that she wanted to serve at the altar with me during the services.

At first, the priests were adamant that she should not be allowed to be an altar girl. Eventually, though, they agreed. I think it was her devotion to the church that persuaded them to change their minds. She was probably one of the first altar girls the Catholic Church allowed. The first in Enid, anyway.

During one of our church services, Amber and I were assisting the priest, as usual, while he took Communion. Suddenly, I saw the church and everything in it move rapidly in a side-to-side and up-and-down motion. The priest's words sounded very slow and clear. I could barely keep standing. I hadn't experienced that feeling before.

The attention of everyone in the church was fixed on me. The priest asked me if I was okay and if I could continue serving. I said that I could.

Later, the priest told me that the unfamiliar feeling had been simply my first experience with nausea and faintness from being in the spotlight. At the time, I accepted this explanation.

But I clearly remember the feeling that I experienced during that service. It was similar to the astral and/or out-of-body experiences (OBE) that I describe later. I now wonder if that feeling was an extraordinary divine experience.

If it was, it might have been another opportunity

for me to learn about my spirit and Ultimate Reality. Unfortunately, instead of opting for learning, I let this opportunity go, just as I did with the "Inky foresight."

For the next three years, I continued to attend church. I spent a lot of time involved in childhood activities, like Little League football.

∽

During the seventh grade, my family and I moved. My parents had decided to leave Enid because the local economy was suffering. But even more so, they realized that Oklahoma could only provide limited opportunities for Amber and me in the future. My parents decided that Denver, Colorado would be a great location.

It took around six months for my father to find a job and a place for us to live in Denver. During this time, Amber and I lived with my grandmother in Beaver, Oklahoma, a small town in the northwestern part of the state. This strip of land is also known as the Oklahoma panhandle. There were no Catholic churches in Beaver, so we stopped attending church.

One night around midnight, my mother was "centering," a technique some in the Catholic Church taught. Centering is a quiet, contemplative state with the focus on finding the center of the soul. Amber and I joined her; it was exciting to stay up that late.

My mother tried to teach us about the importance of a quiet time for the spirit. But my sister and I did not really understand what we were doing. I became impatient, and gave up.

Once more, I had passed up an opportunity to learn about my spirit.

~

As summer approached, my father got his affairs in order so we could move to Colorado. We moved to Littleton, a suburb near Denver. This is where I started the eighth grade.

As I mentioned already, my family and I had stopped attending church. This didn't bother me, though, because I was busy being a kid.

The kids at junior high in Littleton were different from those I had known in any of the schools in Oklahoma. All of a sudden, it was essential to be in a social group and have a circle of friends around you. I had not experienced that in Beaver or Enid. Because I didn't know anyone and had an accent, many of the kids were mean to me. Our recent move had also left me feeling insecure.

As I attended the eighth and ninth grades, I kept expecting God to make the kids at school stop tormenting me. But it never happened; at least, not to my satisfaction. Because of this, I began to think that God didn't exist.

By the time I went to high school, I had only a few friends, and many kids still teased me. I was at the point where I stopped caring about receiving an education. Under peer pressure, I even used drugs. God and religion were nowhere to be seen in my life.

I managed to graduate, but my grades were far below average. My only choice for post-secondary education was a community college with a lower admission requirement than the major colleges or universities.

My intelligence was not the problem. Earlier, when I was in the second grade, I had had the third-highest IQ score of all elementary school children in Stillwater.

At community college, I took geology, chemistry, and anthropology. The study of historical geology and evolution in anthropology further convinced me there was not a God. I began to tell people that I was an atheist. I thought I had enough facts to make that decision.

~

CHAPTER 5

Depression and the Magic of Music

BY THE TIME I GRADUATED from high school, I was lost. I certainly did not know what I wanted to "do" with my life. The depression from years of mean treatment and being made fun of at school still lingered. My last two years of high school were all right, but I was smoking marijuana frequently and did not care about my grades.

Nor did I care about going to college. The only jobs I was qualified for seemed "mindless" and unpleasant, like working at a fast-food place.

This had been the worst part of my life so far. It was governed by an overwhelming sense of hopelessness. I look back now and I can't see a big problem at the source of this hopelessness. But at that time, I didn't know if those feelings would ever pass.

Again, I was expecting God to come and fix my life. I kept waiting, but God did not seem to want to help me. This was the key reason I called myself an atheist.

A few months later, Jeff, a good friend from high school, came to visit me. But his visit was more than just a visit. He had no place to stay.

His life seemed worse than mine. He did have a minimum-wage job, but he couldn't afford to live on his own. Perhaps the worst thing was he was a heavy drug user. However, I convinced my parents to let him stay with us. I know now that part of the reason they let him stay was for my benefit. He lived with us for almost a year. In a way, we helped each other with our struggles just by being friends to one another.

Soon after Jeff moved in with us, he took advantage of our hospitality. One day, he stole some valuable coins from my family and a small pistol from me. My father and I enjoyed collecting and shooting guns—this was the reason I had a pistol. I would never use a gun in a harmful way.

I was not happy about the latter theft in particular, mostly because I was concerned that he might shoot someone while he was high on drugs.

When he came home early the next morning, I confronted him. I was scared because I knew he had a gun. My gun. So I put my other pistol in my pocket.

It was loaded. I now know that this was a stupid thing to do. But I was young, and doing this gave me a sense of power.

I demanded that he give back the coins and the gun. For the first time since I had known him, I had a serious talk with him. I told him that he was on the wrong track in life. I even said that if he kept this up, he could end up dead. He listened to me that night, but it still took him a couple of years to clean up his act.

~

Anyway, Jeff had brought an old electric guitar with him when he moved in. He taught me a few chords. I always loved music; I had spent time playing the cello and the piano previously. So I pushed myself to learn the guitar. Every night when Jeff went to work, I went up to his room to play his guitar.

Two months later, his car broke down. The carburetor needed to be replaced. Since he was spending most of his money on drugs, marijuana mostly, he couldn't afford a new carburetor. I bought the carburetor for him. It was $106. I told him that he could pay me back by buying me a new electric guitar (cheap ones were about $100), without expecting that he would actually buy me a guitar. But, in the back of my mind, I was hoping he would.

About a week later, he did bring home a new guitar for me. I immediately bought a couple of guitar books so I could learn more than the few chords I already knew. After that, Jeff and I spent a lot of time playing our guitars, although neither one of us was very good.

I gradually became obsessed with my guitar. After a while, I thought I was ready to have formal instruction. Fortunately, I found a good teacher and my parents paid for lessons.

During my first two years of college, I took classes in music history and theory. I aced those classes. I joined the college rock band and spent many hours playing the guitar.

For my last two years of college, I transferred to Metropolitan State College of Denver (MSCD), a four-year college. When I first enrolled, I chose music as my minor. To my surprise, the time I had spent with music paid off when I was awarded a scholarship for my classical guitar skills. I planned on becoming a concert guitarist.

I majored in geography, which I chose even though I had failed it in high school. The geography degree I was working toward was focused on environmental science and natural resource conservation, something that appealed to me.

A couple of months later, I decided to change my

major to music. I began to practice my classical guitar more than ever, often eight to ten hours a day.

My practicing proved to be too much physically, however, and my body let me know it. I acquired tendonitis so badly in both arms that I had to give up my collegiate music career and my dreams of being a professional musician. I went back to my original choice and received a degree in geography instead.

∾

I did not realize it at the time, but the guitar and my love for music were given to me by God. Although I still considered myself an atheist, God had answered my prayers and made me happy about my life.

Fortunately, Jeff also found a way to get on the right path. For him, it was the Mormon Church. He tried to get me to join, but I resisted. I still wanted nothing to do with God.

CHAPTER 6

~

My Ascent and the
End of the Rainbow

DURING THE LAST YEAR I attended MSCD, I relaxed my religious—or non-religious—views a bit. In other words, I began to ease up about calling myself an atheist.

I realized that if there was a God, then I was not being fair with Him (or Her). So I changed my views from atheist to agnostic. Simply put, I went from believing that there was no God to proclaiming, "I don't know if there is a God."

By now, I could play each instrument in a rock band, although I wasn't particularly skilled. And I had learned enough about music theory to write reasonably good music.

I decided to write music that would express my feelings. First, I wanted to express how I thought God was supposed to come and help me during high school and after. I wrote a song called "My Ascent." The lyrics follow. The *You* I refer to is God.

Verse 1:	*Darkness, all around me,*
	I feel, it's going to get me
	Can You, only help me?
Verse 2:	*I walk, in the shadows,*
	Will You, ever find me?
	Will I be, lost forever?
Chorus 1:	*To unlock my life,*
	You, You hold the key
	Please let me rise,
	You, You'll set me free
	Through all of this,
	I am still waiting, waiting, waiting,
	For my ascent
Verse 3:	*Now I, I feel I know You,*
	But no, I'll never show You
	In my life, You've broken promises

Verse 4:   *Must I, pray for You,*
              Did You, help me through?
              It's now time for You to go

Chorus 2:   *I unlocked my life,*
              I, I held the key
              I let me rise,
              And I set me free

              Through all of this,
              I am still watching, watching, watching,
              My ascent

When I wrote this song, I firmly believed that God had nothing to do with me putting my life back in order.

∾

A few months later, I wrote a song that described my feelings at the time. I called it "The End of the Rainbow."

Legend says that there are riches at the end of the rainbow. At that point in my life, the "pot of gold," for me, was "the meaning of life." What follow are the lyrics to "The End of the Rainbow."

My Ascent and the End of the Rainbow

Verse 1:   I've come so far just to see,
             Lightning bolts and roses to cover me
             I'll never find a way to let this rest,
             A journey so hard, just a test

Verse 2:   Time in itself means nothing,
             I've lost control of mind and body,
             My visions lie on the edge of a dream
             But I have no way to cleanse them
             From me

Chorus: Now I think I've found…
             The end of the rainbow,
             Like nothing I've ever seen
             The end of the rainbow,
             It's all I've ever dreamed

Verse 3:   Still I'm searching for my destiny,
             Throughout the land
             And across the seven seas
             Where is the place for my soul?
             Will it always be there to shelter me?

Verse 4:   When darkness falls it's so cold,
             The flames are there,

But give me no warmth
When I finally find my escape,
I won't hesitate to cry. . .

Clearly, I was searching for something when I wrote this song. I knew it was possible that God was what I was searching for. But I was not about to search for God.

For the next four years, I concentrated on my career in geography and Geographic Information Systems (GIS). I also learned computer programming on my own to increase my career skills. For most of that time, I was comfortable as an agnostic.

≈

CHAPTER 7

From Agnostic to Gnostic

IN EARLY 1999, I STARTED to search for something more. I had an empty feeling in my heart. I needed something to believe in to help me get through life.

This emptiness was brought about largely by my physical condition. (In the next chapter, I describe this condition in depth.)

I was in a bookstore one day and found a book called *The Occult*, a general overview of supernatural and magical beliefs. I decided to buy the book, because I hoped to find something great in it.

But later, I found that I was hesitant to read it. When finally I did, I spent only about one hour reading various parts of it. I read about Aleister Crowley, black magic, Satanism, and malevolent witchcraft.

I despised most of the things I read. I saw little that was good in the entire content of that book.

I had a definite strange feeling as I read, as if I had to force myself to continue. I believe now that my spirit was being led away from reading more. Today, I'm grateful for that guidance.

∿

In the late summer of 1999, when I was 28, I went on a sea fishing trip with my father, Amber, and her husband. We drove from Denver, Colorado to Vancouver, British Columbia, Canada. I could not wait for that long and boring drive to end. The drive was filled with beautiful scenery, however, and I enjoyed that.

At the start of our drive, Amber pulled out a book called *Adventures of a Psychic* by Sylvia Browne. We talked a little about the book, but at that point I thought it was just more occult stuff. I remember thinking, "What is my sister into now?"

When finally we arrived in Vancouver, we drove our truck aboard a large ferry to reach Vancouver Island, about an hour and a half across the Strait of Georgia. From the ferry terminal at Nanaimo on Vancouver Island, we drove for a few hours to Campbell River, a town halfway up the east side of Vancouver Island. We fished near Campbell River, not in the open waters of the Pacific, but in the Strait of Georgia between Vancouver Island and the Canadian mainland. At night, we slept in our boat, moored to the marina in Campbell River.

One night, after a rather unsuccessful day of fishing, my father, my brother-in-law and I encouraged Amber to read aloud from her "psychic" book.

We were really just encouraging her so that we could laugh at what she read. She read some sentences and we did laugh. But, as I went to sleep in the bow of that boat, I thought, "There is something worth exploring in what my sister has just read to us."

~

After we returned home to Denver, I went to a bookstore to buy that book. I wanted to learn why *Adventures of a Psychic* was a best-seller.

While I was in the store, I looked at the new releases. I saw a book by the same author entitled *The Other Side and Back*. So I bought this instead of the one I had set out to buy.

Yet somehow I was in no hurry to read this book, though I had gone to the trouble to buy it. I did read the front and back cover, though, and spent enough time looking at the author's picture for it to make a strong impression on my mind.

A few days later, my father and I took a drive in a car I had just purchased. Since we were in a part of the Denver metropolitan area we normally don't visit, we stopped in at a local sporting goods store. My father wanted to buy a new hunting rifle.

He bought the gun and then had to wait about 40 minutes while the store clerk did a background check on him, a background check required by law. During this time, two people came into the store. One was a young man in his 20s or 30s and the other a woman about 40.

As I sat there waiting, she turned and looked at me. Her facial features were remarkably similar to those of Browne, the author of *The Other Side and Back*. For a second, I could feel my heart sink in an oddly surreal way.

I believe that this was a divine signal to encourage me to read the book. I wonder now if it was the same force that had previously turned me away from the occult book.

Anyway, it worked. In a way, the whole experience scared me, but, at the same time, I became excited at what I might find in the book.

That night, I began reading at 7 and did not stop until after 11. As I read, many of the deep feelings I had when I was a young churchgoer came rushing back to me. I was awestruck. What I was reading was so spiritual, yet so free of any religious dogma. An example from the book reads, "Because we're part of Him just as He is part of us, there is no such thing as getting 'closer' to Him—we're already there." In this quote, "Him" and "He" refers to God.

This outlook on spirituality was new to me. I had not been exposed to it through the Catholic or Lutheran religions, and I certainly had not found it in my brief exploration of the occult.

That night, I knew a door had been opened and enlightenment awaited. I knew immediately I had found what I had been searching for. And it turned out that what I was searching for was God, although I hadn't realized it previously. This time, I decided to embrace my spirituality, God and our Ultimate Reality with a passion I had never before known. It was the greatest night of my life up until then.

Starting from that night, I was an agnostic no more. As usual, I needed to label my belief. The opposite of agnosticism is gnosticism; this is based upon the Greek word gnosis, which simply refers to knowledge and a sense of knowing. So I saw the word "gnostic" as appropriate for me.

Part 2

≈

My Divine Journey

~

CHAPTER 8

My Blessed Handicap

BEGINNING IN 1997, when I was 26, I started to lose a significant amount of physical coordination and balance. It gradually became difficult to walk; sometimes, I even fell. At the request of my doctor, in 1999 I had an MRI (Magnetic Resonance Image) taken of my brain.

The MRI indicated atrophy of part of my brain, of the cerebellum. I promptly set up an appointment with a neurological specialist.

In an attempt to diagnose my condition, this specialist subjected me to every applicable blood and genetic test available. But each test came back with normal results.

Consequently, the specialist could not diagnose my condition, other than to say that I had ataxia.

Ataxia is a general term used to describe coordination problems such as unsteady balance, awkward movements, and difficulty walking. In some cases, the cause of these symptoms is diagnosed as being genetic. Such a diagnosis usually means that the disease is progressive. Probably the most common form is Friedreich's Ataxia. But when the root cause cannot be traced genetically, the word "ataxia" merely describes the symptoms of an unknown condition.

There is no significant treatment for this disorder; at least, not one that the medical profession can provide. It is a reality check when trained neurological doctors throw their hands up and say, "I don't know" when trying to diagnose and/or treat this condition. I have seen two neurological specialists about my ataxia, and both of them told me straight up that they could not help me.

The bottom line is that the medical profession can't tell me why I have this condition, how to treat it, or if it will get any worse. Likely, it will get worse—atrophy of the cerebellum is generally progressive.

However, medical science, in the form of stem-cell research, does hold some hope for ataxia sufferers. There is increasing evidence that stem cells can treat and possibly cure the cause of ataxia and other degenerative neuromuscular diseases. Stem cells might be able to use their adaptive growth characteristics to compensate for damaged cells.

~

Most doctors and physical therapists agree that physical exercise is the best way to fight ataxia and, possibly, stave off progressive cerebellar degeneration. So about eight months after I had my initial MRI, I started to work out at a gym close to my house. Working out or any equivalent physical exercise is, for me, a chore at any time, not just after a day of work. Simply walking is a struggle for me. It was not easy to exercise, but I knew it was necessary.

One evening, I went to the gym to work out for 40 minutes or so. I had almost finished when a young man of about 30 approached me.

He said, "I normally would not do this, but. . ." It seemed odd that he had singled me out and approached me. But what came out of his mouth next really surprised me.

He said he had been across the gym riding an exercise bike and watching me walk. He told me he had immediately thought, "That poor guy has to put up with this all day long." He then went on to tell me how he had recently been diagnosed with MS—multiple sclerosis. He said that he knew what I was going through.

We started to talk, and I told him that my specialist could not help me with a diagnosis. He asked me who my specialist was. When I told him, he said that mine was the same one he had first gone to, and he could not get a diagnosis, either. He had gotten a second opinion and encouraged me to do likewise.

I started telling him about my work. He jumped in and told me that he worked at IBM. About two hours earlier, I had sent my resume to IBM to see if that company might have an opening that I was qualified for. (I was always on the lookout for what I thought would be a better job than the one I had.)

I told him that I played guitar but was not as good as I had been before my physical problems manifested. He said that he, too, played guitar and had the same problem.

We talked a bit more before he had to leave. I asked him what his regular workout schedule was. He told me, and I assured him I would see him again, as his schedule was similar to mine.

I worked out at this club for another six weeks, until I found a cheaper place to go. I went at the times when he said he would be there, but I never saw him again.

Something about him had seemed unusual, other than the fact that what he had said seemed to be an extension of my own problems. There might have been a perfectly logical reason why I never saw him again, like his MS having progressed to a point where he was not physically able to work out. Or he may have been an angel that had temporarily taken human form to help me.

Regardless, his message to me was divine. It was a message of compassion and understanding. What he had said to me that night made me feel happy and much more content about my life. He helped me realize what others go through and that I was not alone. I had met someone, outside of my family and close friends, who sympathized with me. Our world truly needs more people like this.

$\sim$

By the summer of 2001, my condition had progressed to the point that my walking was seriously impaired. The best way to describe how it looked is to compare it with the staggering of a drunk.

I could no longer jog or run. I would frequently have dreams in which I could move my body like I had in the past. In these dreams, I thought, "See, this is easy. What's my problem?"

During that summer, I finally found a new position in Geographic Information Systems (GIS), my current career. For six months before that, I had been working as a consultant but looking for a permanent position.

I had been on about 20 job interviews. I was qualified for the positions I interviewed for. But when my interviewers would see me walk, they always found a reason not to hire me. It was frustrating, especially because although I could learn new skills, there was nothing I could do about the way I walked.

Anyway, I was grateful when I was offered a new job. I had medical insurance once again.

All along, my intuition told me that a second opinion about my medical condition would not help my situation. But, as I became more desperate for a diagnosis, I believed a more accurate diagnosis might possibly help me. I knew that chances were slim. This triggered my decision to see another neurological specialist and get a second opinion, as the young man at the gym had suggested.

This specialist did everything he could to arrive at a diagnosis. He wanted me to take some newly developed genetic tests. Unfortunately—or fortunately—the results of these tests were normal.

The specialist then looked at my then two-year-old MRI. He examined it with a group of radiologists in the hospital's radiology lab. The long wait in the examining room was my first clue to what they were thinking. My specialist came back and told me that all of the radiologists were "impressed" by my MRI.

It is true that my condition is rare. But I was not exactly happy to learn that the radiologists were excited at my difficult situation. In fact, I became upset. When I calmed down and returned to rational thought, I understood that they were only excited because they had never seen an MRI quite like mine.

∽

In March of 2003, I finally received divine guidance concerning my ataxia. It happened one afternoon while I was relaxing. I brought it about while feeling rather depressed, and, speaking honestly, I really needed this experience. To this day, I thank God for it.

Before I describe this experience, I want to explain what I meant above by, "I brought it about." In the time leading up to this point, I kept saying to God that I was sick and tired of my ataxia. I also said that the thought of a future with this condition was overwhelming.

I believe our spirits are always connected to God. When words of desperation are involved, I believe that God responds quickly. This is what happened:

About a year and a half after starting my new job, I attended a business conference. The hotel where it was held was quite large, and this put me in a situation where I had to do a lot of walking.

I know from experience that walking is an automatic

and pleasant experience for most people, just as it once was for me.

But, by this time, walking had become a chore, and the truth is that I did not look forward to it and avoided it whenever possible. If I made one false move while walking, I could lose my balance and risk injuring myself from either running into something or falling. It took a lot of energy for me to guard against this happening, and I tired easily. All this is part of my life even now.

This particular day in March, I was so tired from all the walking that I had to go back to my hotel room to try to take a nap. I was also feeling sorry for myself. I felt like this because my life was so much more difficult physically than it needed to be.

Anyhow, I laid down on the bed. About ten minutes later, I felt a type of vibrating sensation, although I was not physically moving, and heard a loud buzzing noise similar to the sound of "snow" on a TV set.

Some call this an astral catalepsy, where the spirit temporarily crosses over to the Other Side, Heaven, or whatever you want to call it.

First, I found myself in a dark and vast emptiness. Ahead of me, I could hear beautiful voices calling to me. A couple of the phrases were, "Brandon, come over here," and "We are waiting for you." What happened next was rather humorous.

I saw a big, circular object before me, like a big yellow beach ball. The surface of the ball was segmented with small squares, similar to the pattern on a volleyball.

On each square was a stick figure like the ones we all drew in grade school. One of the stick figures said, "Brandon, we need your help. Will you help us?" I said, "Of course I will. I love you." I instantly found myself in the entryway of a house.

The house looked like an ordinary house that a small family would live in. A woman was there to greet me. She then took me on a tour of the house. Every now and then she would stop and tell me what was wrong at that location in the house. The problems at the places we stopped were not structural, and I can't explain what they were. But I could feel some uneasiness at these places.

At each stop, she said, "This is the problem. Can you fix it, and how will you fix it?" I don't recall the exact words of my response, but I told her that yes, I could fix these problems and explained how I could fix them.

After this, I opened my eyes. As I lay in bed, I felt great. For the next few hours, I had lots of spiritual and mental energy. My physical condition, though, did not change.

I'm not sure if this experience was presenting me

with another opportunity to permanently leave this world. But it did help give me the courage and strength to carry on with life and do the best I could.

My life is still difficult physically. And not a day goes by when I don't wish that my condition would leave me.

∼

Much of the remainder of this book is based on my personal daily affirmations. I call them affirmations, but they could be called personal prayers or even mantras. Many people say something similar to these to themselves or to a higher power, such as God.

I have included the relevant portion of these at the beginning of each appropriate chapter, and I include them in their entirety at the end of the book.

~

CHAPTER 9

The Handicap
We All Face

"Let my higher self rise to the place where it should be today. I want to function from there. Also, help me to prevent my lower self from unduly influencing me."

THROUGHOUT MY LIFE, I've always expected various experiences in life to be more fulfilling than they actually are. I know it might sound strange, but often my new experiences end with me saying, "Is that it?" I think this is common to many of us.

For example, the professional fireworks displays I've seen are extremely beautiful. But all I could do was just watch them. Yet I always wanted somehow to be one with the fireworks and actually feel their glory.

In my affirmations, I ask God to help me function from my higher self. My "higher self" is a less scientific name for the superconscious area of my mind. But I also believe that the superconscious is more than just a mental realm. I like to think it is a connection to the spirit and to God.

This affirmation helps me not to be petty when I interact with others. It aligns me with the real essence of my spirit. I can go to work and let things go when the meetings, responsibilities, stress, and bureaucracy become overwhelming. And most of all, this alignment helps me cope with and appreciate life.

∼

A few months after I started to say affirmations daily, I found an opportunity to speak with a well-known psychic. My time with this person was brief, so I asked just one question: "Why do I have such poor balance?"

The psychic's reply was, "You are too sixth-sensory." I interpreted this to mean that I am too focused or fixated on my sixth sense rather than on my five "earthly" senses. If this is true, then the higher-self portion of my affirmations might have been having a substantial effect on me. And believing this gave me courage. Courage to know that I was controlling my life for the better. I was, and still am, trying to live this way.

I know that I need to be grounded in this world while I'm here. But I also know that I will never give up my sixth sense, something I've worked so hard at developing and something I'll continue to fortify.

So my challenge is to balance my human life on earth with a spiritual life, a life not directly dependent on this world. The human and the spiritual are two different things. But I also believe that, with concerted effort, they can be made into one and the same. Balance isn't a given, be it physical, mental, or spiritual—it's a gift.

I believe that this challenge of balancing the lower self with the higher didn't single out just me. It singled out all of us. And, in a real way, it might be what we all want to achieve while we're here in this world.

~

CHAPTER 10

Less than Ideal Moments

A FEW YEARS AGO, Jeff, the friend I mentioned in chapter 5, asked me to go with him and his wife to the local renaissance fair, held annually in the rolling foothills of the Colorado Front Range, close to the town of Larkspur, near Colorado Springs.

I knew immediately that it would probably be difficult for me to walk, as mountainous terrain is usually uneven. An uneven walking surface is difficult for me, because I have a hard time dealing with the gradient variations. But because it was about a month away and I had never been to the fair, I told myself, "I will deal with any hardships. It's no big deal." I contacted Jeff and agreed to go.

Before the date, I arranged for my friend, Sheila, to

join us. When the day arrived, we drove to Larkspur and the fair.

The land was beautiful, as are most foothills and mountains. We had to walk about a third of a mile along a scenic footpath to get to the entry of the fair.

Everything was going fine until we got about half way. The trail then followed a small hill. I had a hard time walking down that 30-foot hill. Luckily, there were trees growing alongside that I was able to hold on to.

I moved slowly. My friends had to wait for me at the bottom of the hill. And my slow walking was an inconvenience to the people behind me. It struck me that some of them were probably thinking, "What in the hell is this guy's problem?"

The rest of the day was a lot of work. It was tiring just to walk while trying not to fall. Fortunately, Sheila helped me to get around.

At the end of the day, I went into one of the shops at the fair. Doing so turned out to be a bad idea. For one thing, I was exhausted by then. For another, the floor had about a three-inch slope. That was enough to catch me off guard. I fell hard. Everyone turned to see what had happened. As it was a wood floor with no carpet, the impact of the fall smarted. I had cut my hand when I braced myself for the fall. I helped myself up and walked out of the shop.

I felt pretty low after that. I had tried so hard that day not to fall. And I remembered that when I'd been younger, an outing like this had always been very enjoyable and posed no problem whatsoever.

Right after I fell, I realized, once again, that this physical condition would continue to affect me for the rest of my life. The thoughts that then ran through my mind were horrible. One such thought was about how, in old age, when physical mobility is limited anyway, my ataxia would further compound the limits of my mobility.

The trip back to my car was hard. I am grateful to Sheila for helping me make it.

The next year, Jeff asked me if I wanted to go to the fair again. Although I did want to, I had to say no, because I knew it would be too difficult.

~

I still have vivid memories of the activities I used to do. I remember the countless hours I spent riding a bike. I remember running, jogging, and even snow skiing. But for the last six or seven years, I have not been able to do any of those things.

I still lapse into a depressed state when I think of what I can't do anymore. I realize that when I do this, I'm being harsh and unfair with myself. I get depressed more often than I would like to, and it bothers me. But I have hope that, with God's help, someday I'll be able to put this negative thinking behind me.

For various reasons, many of us, at least the people I've met, get episodes of depression from time to time. Such episodes can be ruthless and cruel. No one deserves them.

Episodic depression can be hard to work through, but I am convinced that it can be completely abolished—with God's help. Today, when these episodes come to me, I just say to myself, "God, please help me. Take this away from me. I don't want this." God always answers my call. This is my sure way to end depression.

∼

CHAPTER II

Intellectual Creation?

"Today, I want the left and right sides, hemi-spheres, of my mind to come together in equilibrium and perfect harmony. Help me to achieve a balance between my intellectual center (left side) and my emotional center (right side)."

No, THE TITLE OF THIS CHAPTER is not from the military intelligence archives. It's about what many call the "left" and the "right" sides of the mind (or brain).

In my affirmations, I say that I want to balance these sides of my mind. According to science, the left side is thought to be where intellectual thought originates and the right side is said to control creativity and emotion.

After saying these affirmations for more than a year,

I went on a mandatory "retreat" for my work. It wasn't quite an "I need a hug" type of deal, but it was close. This was a new experience for me.

I currently work for the Colorado State Government. I don't know why we went on this "retreat." Maybe someone thought it would be good for our work environment. Whether this retreat has had an effect on my work remains unclear, but I did get something specific out of it.

Before going on the retreat, we were supposed to answer some questions, as instructed by management. These questions were posted on a website by a company that claimed it could analyze the answers to the questions and tabulate meaningful results. I don't remember the specific questions, but I do recall the overall nature of them and how the multiple choices were organized. Here are examples of the type of questions we were asked.

1. If a co-worker verbally abused you, would you:
   A. Tell management about it
   B. Confront the person
   C. Do a combination of A and B
   D. Get even

   or

2. If you had to drive somewhere you had never been before, would you:
   A. Read a map
   B. Ask for directions
   C. Do a combination of A and B
   D. Just start driving

Most people in the office, including myself, thought these questions were rather silly. But although we were saying "whatever" to ourselves, we did answer the questions.

At the retreat, the company that was hired to facilitate had analyzed our answers and tabulated the results. The 30 or so questions with our individual answers were supposed to indicate how our minds worked. In other words, the results were meant to measure individual cognitive processes.

The company prepared a pie chart for everyone. The mind was represented as a circle, with 50 percent being the left side and the other 50 being the right. The company took this pie chart one step further, though, by breaking the left half into two equal, 25-percent segments; one piece representing analytical thought and the other structural thought. The right half was also divided equally, into conceptual thought and social thought.

Everyone received one of these pie charts. Each one

of our answers to the initial questionnaire was worth a small percentage value on the chart. Based on the answer given to any specific question, the percentage value was marked in one of the four quadrants: analytical, structural, conceptual, or social thought.

My results were close to equal for each quadrant. According to this profile, 25 percent for each thought category was a perfect score. Specifically, my breakdown was 27, 27, 24, and 22 percent. Most of my co-workers had much more unequal results.

According to the company that did the analysis, only one percent of the population has a cognitive process similar to mine. So, according to this analytical process, I don't follow the norm. This wasn't exactly news to me—after all, I can't walk straight for more than five feet.

As soon as I saw the graph of my mind, I thought that my affirmation, the one about balancing the right and left sides of my mind, was making a significant difference in my life. Seeing the graph made me happy, because I thought that the results were a manifestation of the divine influence in my life. What made me happiest was my assumption that if this one affirmation was helping me, then all of the other ones must also be making a difference.

This graph analysis might have been rather light-hearted—I'm not sure how much truth there really was to it. But I understand that it was a decent attempt to qualify the mind, to make some sense of the variety of cognitive processes we humans have.

≈

In this world, we are encouraged to develop our intellect (left side) to a high degree. I see this most with our system of formal scholastic education. But, unfortunately, we do not do the same for creativity development (right side). Many people are quick to say that being too sensitive and emotional is counterproductive, but I almost never hear the same argument for someone that is too intellectual.

I deeply admire a Native American phrase, "to walk in balance on the Earth Mother." I believe that this refers to spiritual, mental, and physical balance. And, although I'm making what feels like great progress, I'm still learning how involved this really is.

~

CHAPTER 12

Send in the Spirit Guides

"Joy, Marcel, and Marilyn, my spirit guides, guide me through this day. Assist me in my decisions and help me through any negative experiences. Help me to make today the best day I can."

I REMEMBER IT LIKE IT WAS YESTERDAY. I was lying in bed around 6 AM, and I asked my spirit guide to come and tell me his or her name.

I then drifted into a light dream state. I visualized driving around my old neighborhood with a friend. At the end of our short drive, we crashed into a wood fence, upon which I heard a loud and clear female voice declare, "My. . .my name is Joy." In that instant, I knew exactly what had happened, and I went with it.

I believe that our spirits or souls always resonate to the truth. And this resonance can be instantaneous. And so I accepted the name "Joy" without second-guessing what I had experienced while in my dreamlike state.

≈

About a year later, however, when Amber and I signed up for a past-life regression, I discovered that I had more than one spirit guide. I had seen an ad on the internet for past life regression and thought it would be fun.

A past life regression (also known as PLR therapy) is a type of hypnosis session with the focus being on recollecting any previous lifetimes or lives of the spirit. I guess my regression was typical. And although at the time it felt a bit like I was just making up stuff, I did explore four of my past lives.

The only lifetime that is really interesting took place in medieval times or the "dark" ages. Basically, I saw myself being killed by a sword on a rocky shoreline. Next, I saw my spirit hovering above a large castle. It came to me that I was in this "hovering about" state for 40 years—I understood that to indicate that my spirit had spent time as a ghost.

≈

Toward the end of regression, my hypnosis guide attempted to take my spirit to the Other Side, or Heaven, or whatever you want to call it, and see God. I'm not totally convinced that we succeeded, but I did have some intense visualizations. This little side trip was not a normal part of a past life regression, and what I'm about to describe has nothing to do with a past life. But it does have something to do with one of my spirit guides, so I've chosen to include it in this chapter. Here is what I saw:

First, I saw myself traveling through the "tunnel" that connects this world to the Other Side. Before I went in the tunnel, my hypnosis [PLR] guide called for one of my spirit guides to come and assist me.

The shape of the spirit that appeared in my visualization was female, and I expected it to be Joy. But this spirit introduced herself as Marilyn. Her introduction was more of a thought than a verbal phrase.

I must have traveled through the tunnel with Marilyn, because my next visual was of a large white building. It was only about a hundred feet wide, but it seemed to be over a thousand feet long. The inside of the building was decorated with what looked like white marble. Chairs and meeting tables lined the walls. At this point, Marilyn had left me.

Only one person—or perhaps he was a spirit—was in that room with me, an older man with long, grayish-white hair and beard. We had a short conversation. He was coaching me on my earthly role, which he communicated to me thus: "You are to help people." I could not glean more information than that.

He told me that I was doing a good job. But he also said that I should do more.

A few moments later, another spirit arrived. He was sitting in a big plush chair that had full armrests. His clothing, a cloak or robe, was entirely black. He had short black hair and a goatee beard. His only communication to me was the pronounced smile he wore.

Perhaps I had actually visited our Ultimate Reality—or perhaps this experience was merely a creation of my mind. Regardless, this image will stay with me for the rest of my life.

I now realized that I had two spirit guides and could address them by name. I had Joy, and I had Marilyn, a name I had liked as a kid—now I knew why.

∽

Before I go on, I want to explain what my idea of "spirit guides" is.

Spirit guides are wonderful blessed entities from Ultimate Reality that assist us through life. A spirit guide always has first-hand experience of life on earth. That is, they have incarnated on earth one or more times. This helps them to know what they are up against when they guide people through this life.

I believe that every person has one or more spirit guides. Some guides communicate verbally, while others rely upon thought infusion. I also believe that many of the "inexplicable" feelings or senses people get are simply communications from their spirit guide(s).

I do not equate spirit guides with guardian angels. I believe that angels are special entities created by God.

~

I could often sense a presence that was, undoubtedly, guiding my spirit, yet I felt strongly that it was neither Joy nor Marilyn. I felt that this presence was more than one soul, and described it to myself as a "collective soul."

I should mention here that this happened soon after I had accepted gnosticism as the belief system closest to my own. As mentioned in chapter 7, gnosticism describes a spiritual belief system with the quest for knowledge—gnosis—at its core. Christian gnosticism blossomed in the years after the crucifixion of Jesus Christ. But gnosticism was also around before that, in so-called "pagan" times.

When I first became gnostic, I walked to work each morning through a city park full of big trees. Almost every morning, I saw one or more squirrels. They collected food and ran from tree to tree.

I knew I could not tell the squirrels apart enough to name each one even though I wanted to, thanks to my "naming obsession." So I came up with a name that I felt applied to all of them: Marcel. Marcel was a collective squirrel soul.

Since the name "Marcel" had meaning to me as a collective soul, I felt it was appropriate for the presence that I sensed was guiding my spirit. I hoped that this spirit guide didn't mind being named after a few park squirrels.

So my three spirit guides are Joy, Marcel, and Marilyn. And I'm grateful for their love and guidance. If you have not met your spirit guide(s) yet, all you have to do is to ask yourself or God to make it happen. I know of no reason why this wouldn't work.

≈

CHAPTER 13

Good Encounters, Bad Encounters

"Jesus, walk with me today. Help me to have
great physical balance. Help me to walk like
I know I can. Protect me from falling and,
possibly, hurting myself."

IN THE SEVEN YEARS that I've had ataxia, I've had some good experiences and what feels like many more bad ones, all to do with my condition. What I really want to talk about here is human compassion, of which, unfortunately, too many people have a serious lack.

When I worked in downtown Denver from 1998–2002, I learned how some people perceive me. Too often, learning this was painful.

One Friday evening after work, I started to walk the four blocks to my car. Friday is the absolute worst day of the week for me, because I get progressively more tired in the course of a workweek. By the time Friday afternoon rolls around, my ataxia is nearly twice as bad as it is on Sunday or Monday.

After two blocks, a man started following me, or so it seemed. Actually, he was just on the same path as me, but, as it turned out, he was also noticing how much difficulty I had as I walked.

When he saw that I was preparing to drive, he started yelling at me, saying that I was in no condition to drive and that I could cause a wreck. He said that if the police had been there, he would have stopped them and told them about me. Finally, he said, "Think about babies." I understood where he was coming from. He thought I was drunk. It is common for people to finish working on Friday and start drinking. And people who have ataxia but are able to walk sometimes seem drunk.

I told this guy more than once that I had not been drinking. It was like talking to a brick wall. He never once stopped to consider what else might cause me to walk the way I did. I soon realized that any further attempt to talk to him would be a lost cause.

Obviously, this did not make me very happy. Our

world is filled with people with this type of mentality. There is not much anyone on the wrong side of it can do to correct it.

~

I had a few more similar experiences, all to do with the seemingly inebriated appearance of my gait. One afternoon when I left work, I walked past three homeless guys sitting on a bench. One of them yelled, "Hey buddy, you heading for detox?" I figured he was referring to me ending up at the detoxification cell in the police department due to what he thought he recognized as my state of apparent inebriation.

~

Another Friday after work, I went to a bar with some co-workers for "happy hour." The waitress refused to serve me because, as she put it, "I was already drunk."

I wanted to respond, to defend myself to her. I thought about the many things, some of them hurtful, I could have said. But in the end, I just let it go.

Since then, I particularly hate being in a bar. Many people look at me like I'm drunk. This is something I have to deal with wherever I go, be it a bar, a restaurant, or even a department store. Because of this misunderstanding, I despise alcohol. I've never liked the taste of it, anyhow, and it just makes my balance that much worse. For me, alcohol is worthless. And a confrontation with a police officer confirmed my distaste for it.

≈

One day on my drive home from work, I stopped at my bank to make a deposit. The parking lot of the bank is near a shopping mall. On my way out of the bank, a nearby police officer spotted me walking. She drove over to my car, then got out and approached me.

I told her about my ataxia, but she did not believe me. She radioed for another officer to come give me a Breathalyzer test. Of course, it was negative. But the initiating officer did not stop there.

She said, "If I could take your licence, I would. You should not be allowed to drive."

She did not attempt to understand what I was telling her. She did not care to listen to reason. For whatever selfish reason, she just wanted to say those unkind things to me.

I can't stop something like this from happening to me again. But, fortunately, one of my doctors wrote a note for me, explaining my ataxia. Now I carry that with me when I drive. And I finally brought myself to use a handicap tag when I park. Hopefully, both of these will help me if I ever find myself in another confrontation with a police officer.

≈

Not everyone thinks I'm drunk, though. Some people think that I am bewitched or possessed. One morning, for example, I was walking the four blocks from my car to my office. Along the way, I passed a black woman. Her physical features made me think that she was not born in the United States or Europe. I guessed that she might have been from Africa.

As I passed her, she started to make faces at me. To this, she added hissing sounds. It was like she was using some incantation, complete with crossed index fingers, to protect herself from me.

It would have been funny, except for the fact that it did not make me feel good. But in hindsight, I think about it and it does make me laugh.

≈

But not all encounters with people I don't know have been bad. For the last two years that I worked in downtown Denver, I commuted on a light rail train. I parked my car at the train stop in my suburb every morning, rode the train downtown, and caught it back at the end of the day.

The train was always filled with many strangers. On two occasions, I fell while walking, once during the morning walk to the station, and once on the way home. Immediately after both these falls, a fellow commuter helped me back to my feet. Both times I gladly took the hands that were offered. I was grateful for the assistance. It is a great feeling to be lifted up by a stranger.

∿

I have met people who never hesitate to offer a helping hand and those who prefer to stare at me and often say something demeaning. Although I'm learning not to be self-conscious about the way I walk, to this day, I wonder what people think when they see me.

∿

I conclude this chapter with one more memory. One afternoon, I left work and started to walk the four blocks to the station. I don't know what spurred me to stray from my usual path, but I soon found myself walking in the wrong direction on a sidewalk alongside a few businesses.

About halfway down the block was a drycleaners. There on the sidewalk in front sat a man. I casually walked by him, somehow expecting, in the back of my mind, that he would stop me and ask for money. To my surprise, when he did stop me, he did not ask for money.

Instead, he said to me, "How are you doing?" I decided to be friendly to the guy, and replied, "Fine. How are you?" He said something like, "Well, I'm back here again for a little while." I think I said, "Oh," or something similar. Next, the conversation took a strange direction.

He said, "Do you remember me? I remember you." I was, and still am, sure I had never seen him before. I replied, "No. No, I don't."

He then started talking about music and how he was a singer for a band. He said he was looking for a guitar player for his band. I felt something lively in the conversation at that point because, as I mentioned previously, music—and especially guitar-playing—was, and still is, very important to me.

I asked, "What are you doing sitting here?" He said that he was trying to collect enough money to buy a can of soda from the soda machine in the drycleaners.

I offered him some change for the soda, but he refused to take it. He said, "You keep your money. I'll be fine." Eventually, I dropped the coins by his side so that he would be tempted to pick them up. Just then, someone came out from the drycleaners and told him to leave.

Later that night, I wondered to whom I had spoken and why he had treated me like a long-lost friend. Earlier, I noticed that he was sitting in an obscure place. A place where I had never seen a homeless person before. It was like he was waiting for me.

Even more perplexing was what he had said. I wondered why he said that he was trying to buy a soda and collect enough change for it, but would not take my money. I had never before noticed a homeless person not taking money when offered it.

Every now and then I think about that conversation, and it always makes me feel good. I did my best to treat this person with kindness and respect. At the time, I felt good that I dropped the coins beside him in order to help him. But after I reflected on this, I began to think that actually he had helped me.

What he did for me I call a divine affirmation. He helped me feel better about myself and he did it without expecting anything from me in return. I'm still very thankful for what this man—or this angel—did.

≈

CHAPTER 14

My Maternal Introduction

"Mother and Father God. . ."

I HAVE A WONDERFUL MOTHER in this world. But this chapter is about someone else. It is about the mother we all have in common—our Mother, God.

During the year and a half that I recited, on a daily basis, the affirmations at the end of this book, I was also reading selected "spiritual" books that were important to me.

My affirmations have always started with, "Mother and Father God." My early religious exposure helped me to learn about and appreciate God, our Father. Although I was bothered by the fact that I was told God was male, I did not question it.

One of the books I was reading introduced me to an age-old concept: the existence of a female God or Goddess. But even though it was ageless wisdom, it was new to me.

It is now my belief that God, our Mother, is the co-creator of the universe. The Mother and the Father come together to form a whole and loving God. Today, when I refer to God, I am always referring to both the Mother and the Father.

When I first learned of the Mother God, I was happy. It made so much sense to me. Shortly thereafter, I was wondering if I could meet Her "in person."

One Saturday, I awoke at 6 AM. I was in a dreamlike state almost identical to the one I'd been in when I first heard Joy's name. My spirit was very peaceful, and I felt well rested. I decided right then that I would call for the Mother God to come and talk to me.

Immediately after I asked this, I closed my eyes and relaxed. I was not fully asleep. Instead of the Mother God coming to talk to me, I was going to talk to her. Like the one described in chapter 8, I was experiencing another astral catalepsy.

After a few seconds of the transition sensation, everything became quiet. I was out of my body at that point. I felt lightweight. I'm almost positive that I traveled to the Other Side, Heaven—Ultimate Reality.

I heard a high-pitched female voice say, "Brandon, I am your Mother." I said, "Hello, I am glad to meet you." And I was.

When I heard the voice, I was extremely happy that my request had been heard. But, at the same time, my spirit and/or body was very uncomfortable. I felt like I still had to breathe but was having a hard time doing so. I was gasping for air. I knew I could barely carry on a conversation. This was disappointing.

Fortunately, we did have a short conversation, as follows. Our Mother said, "Brandon, tell me, what is in the cards?" I was having so much trouble breathing that I could hardly think what to say. My response was not intelligible. I should have asked Her what she meant, but hindsight is always 20/20.

Anyway, all that I could think of when She said "cards" was a playing-card deck (something I don't know a lot about). I said, "Well, there is a king and a queen, and also there is an ace which can be worth one or 13 points, or it can be a wildcard." Later, I thought about what I said and could not think of a card game in which an ace is worth 13 points.

After my reply, I felt I could not breathe, like being underwater with no oxygen left in my lungs. I had heard that an astral experience could seem frightening. Only now do I realize that there is nothing to be afraid of.

I cut the conversation off abruptly, though, and fell back into my body. I did not want to go back into my body. And I felt bad as I was doing it. The worst part is that my fear caused me to abort what was perhaps the most spiritual or psychic experience I will ever have. To this day, I regret cutting off that conversation. But I do know that what I experienced was blessed and divine.

I cherish the memory of that experience. It gave me a real taste of the world beyond this one. And I am convinced that I actually spoke with our Mother God.

I hope that one day I will speak with Her under similar circumstances and be strong enough to hang on much longer. I'm currently working on building that strength.

~

CHAPTER 15

My Own Allegory

IN THE FALL OF 2000, I was visiting a couple of bookstores regularly, hoping to find a particular book of ancient religious writings. I now buy most of my books over the internet, but back then I was resisting online commerce.

The book I was seeking was one I had learned about from reading other books that referred to it: The Nag Hammadi Library (TNHL).

TNHL is a collection of short religious writings. Theologians estimate that these writings are from between the second and fifth centuries AD, although this is not certain. The writings were unearthed in 1945 near a town named Nag Hammadi, in Upper Egypt. These original manuscripts are fragmentary in many places and ellipsis dots (. . .) with square brackets indicate the lacuna (missing portions of text). An example would be, "I am the one who is called Truth, and iniquity [. . .]"

Many theologians attribute most of these writings with gnosticism. Because, as a gnostic, I was on a quest for spiritual knowledge, I had a strong interest in finding a book that was foundational to gnosticism.

After looking for the book for a couple of weeks, I eventually found it. I took it home immediately and started reading. But I soon realized I was having difficulty understanding it. I was reading all these words, but many were not registering.

Then I had a dream that seemed to clarify much of what I had read so far. This dream helped me to put into perspective and understand the words whose meaning had at first escaped me.

~

My dream began with me being in a vast open field of tall grass with a forest a few hundred yards away. As I wandered in this field, I came upon a staircase that extended far underground. It seemed like there were at least a hundred steps. I began to descend. When I reached the bottom, a man was there to greet me. There was not much light down there. And I wondered why I had come to this place.

This man led me into a cavern on my immediate left. Here I saw lots of people, but they seemed unhappy. I could sense this from their blasé facial expressions and apparent lack of motivation.

As my escort and I walked, he explained to me where I was. This was a gathering place for people that, for whatever reason, were not happy.

We then stopped to see a crowd of people gathered around a person in battle armor. Nearby was a large open fire. I asked, "What is that?" His response was odd, something I did not understand at the time of the dream and for a long time after. He said, "That is a political legion." Whatever this was, it seemed to emanate something evil, and I was not about to approach it.

The cavern was a dark and dismal place, and I could not wait to leave. Seeing the political legion was the last straw. I told my escort, "I have seen enough. Lead me out of here." We walked back to the entrance, and he left me.

As I was leaving that place, I noticed that directly across from it was what I thought was another cavern. These caverns were separated by a road or trail.

I walked across this divide and went through the opening of the other cavern. I found a beautiful open area with trees and lots of light. I walked down a central path for a while. With all the lush green vegetation and running water, I thought to myself, this is a very beautiful place.

After I had walked on the central path for about five hundred feet, I came upon a group of people dressed in white robes. They were gathered around a small wood box. They acted as if whatever was inside the box was very important.

When I approached them, they opened the box to show me what was inside. It was a copy of TNHL. This was their secret treasure.

I then turned to leave. I headed back toward the staircase that would take me back up to the field from which I had started. As I left, all the people in white robes started to follow me.

As I came to the exit of this cave-like area, I saw the entrance to the dark cavern I had been in earlier. To my surprise, as I passed the dark place, some of the most unhappy people came out and started to follow me and the people in the white robes.

I arrived at the staircase and started to ascend it. All the people behind climbed with me. In this way, we reached the vast field at the top of the stairs.

When I awoke, I realized that my dream must have had a powerful message for me, but I could not come up with a substantial interpretation. For the next month

I continued to read TNHL. But even after having the dream, I still had to make a concerted effort to comprehend every small nuance as I finished reading the book.

From this point on, however, the words I read in the book were clearer to me. By the time I finished, I felt like I understood what it was really about. Even though I did not understand my dream, I felt that it had helped me to understand the content in TNHL.

∽

About a year later, I went to work on a Saturday. I don't enjoy working on the weekend but help out when someone comes up with a "deadline."

While my software program was processing data, I surfed the internet and found a website dedicated to the writings of the ancient Greek philosopher Plato. I had never read any of his writings. I did take a high school Greek mythology course. What little I learned in that class was all I knew of ancient Greece. On this website, however, there were so many writings available by Plato, I decided to just pick one, thinking that I might find something interesting.

After reading a couple of pages, I quickly made a connection between what he had written and what was in TNHL. To me, Plato's teachings are, at the core, gnostic.

I chose another of his writings and continued to read. What I found was something that interpreted the dream just described in a more or less accurate fashion.

The second piece of writing I found is known as "The Allegory of the Cave" and is from Plato's book *The Republic*. Here Plato presents an analogy for people that are trapped in a material reality and cannot see past it. "The Allegory" is about people who have brought about a personally binding and limiting reality.

Plato begins by describing people who are trapped in a dark cave with a large fire looming next to them. He then says the people can barely turn their heads away from the direct view of the fire. All the while the fire is positioned to cast their shadows on the cave wall. They are sitting there seeing these shadows and, subsequently, believing that the shadows are their true reality.

Plato writes that these people will never know their true reality unless they begin to search for and find the light at the entrance of the cave. The light alludes to a way out of the cave. And the light originates from a type of superreality.

Although the dream I described earlier was not exactly the same as what Plato had described, I still made a connection between the two. To me, my dream had a lot in common with "The Allegory."

In my dream, I was in the dark cave. I even saw the

fire. The first cave I went in was filled with hopelessness; at least, that is what I sensed. My exploring the cave-like area directly across from the first cave symbolized my search for the light that reveals the superreality. Perhaps the people in the white robes and the sight of TNHL helped me find my way back to a better place.

The field at the top of the stairs represents Ultimate Reality, similar to the superreality to which Plato referred.

And, by the way, the political legion I came across might have represented the trap of material reality, much like Plato's description of human silhouettes that were just shadows on the cave's wall.

There was a reason I could remember my dream an entire year after having it. When I came across "The Allegory" and compared it with my dream, I felt like I was fulfilling my destiny. I also felt that this helped me expand my mind and my spirit in the right direction.

This might have been a milestone in my life, or another lesson from which to learn. Whatever it was, it had a positive impact on me. I believe that experiences like this happen to us all. And when they do, our spirit connection to a divine higher power grows stronger.

Part 3

≈

The Everyday Spiritual Quest

≈

CHAPTER 16

Spirit Gazing on
Clear and Cloudy Nights

I LOOK FORWARD TO EVERY NIGHT, because I know that I'm in for a period of rest. Each night is a time when I rejuvenate my mind, body, and spirit.

When I turn off my bedside lamp and lie in bed, I usually see small sparkles of light all around my peripheral field of vision. A good analogy here is to imagine pinpricks through the darkness, allowing little beams of white light to shine through temporarily. I see these beams sparkle whether I keep my eyes open or closed. I'm now to the point where I hope, if not expect, to see these sparkling beams when I lie down to rest.

One odd thing, though, is that when I directly focus my eyes on these white lights, they usually fade away very quickly. So I try to view them mostly from my peripheral vision. That way, they stay around longer.

Maybe I am seeing them from my "third eye" or brow chakra, an energy center located on the forehead immediately above the brow.

I am now convinced that these lights are angels and spirits that come around me at night. Parapsychology and metaphysics have coined the term *orb* for similar little circles of light. Whether or not what I am seeing qualify as orbs, sometimes these beams of white light do seem to react to what I say.

I might say, for example, "I would like for those spirits who love me and whom I love to come into this room." Then I sometimes see two to three times as many lights. Maybe I'll get tired of opening up my room to these spirits in the future, but the novelty has not yet worn off. It is entertaining—for a few minutes each night, anyway.

One important note here is this. When I say, "Who love me and whom I love," I'm filtering out those spirits that have no good reason to come around me. A blanket statement like this does the trick of keeping such spirits from unduly influencing my life. I strongly believe, and I have heard others say this, that when we involve ourselves with the spirit world, we risk being influenced by those spirits that don't really care about us. Although I don't think there is any way they can physically harm us, it's best to keep them at a distance.

Sometimes I see a faint maroon light. Although I don't know "who" that is, I can say that it is special to me.

At times—that is, if I remember to—I ask the archangels to surround me. I know the main constituent of archangels to be Michael, Gabriel, Uriel, and Raphael. I ask each to stand by one of the four sides of my bed as I sleep.

A couple of years ago, I came up with a name for an angel or group of angels, that I thought was pretty good. So I figured I would use it to identify my own angel(s). The name is "Shamaliel." When I remember to ask for the archangels, I ask Shamaliel to accompany them.

~

I have included this chapter, not only to reveal more about my eccentric nature, but to introduce and support the subject of the next chapter: dream programming.

~

CHAPTER 17

The Wonderful World
of Dream Programming

I FIRMLY BELIEVE THAT DREAMS, like computers, can be programmed. I don't believe this because I've read about it; I believe this because I've done it.

Dream programming is a technique that can help us all receive information that is not of this world. Sometimes this information proves to be invaluable to us as we endure this life. Besides, it is fun to do.

Science has given us the term lucid dreaming. A *lucid dream* is one in which the dreamer becomes "conscious" while in his/her dream. In such a dream, the dreamer has learned to control the dream for his/her benefit. Lucid dreaming is a great technique, but there is another, equally effective way to work with dreams.

In this chapter, I explain how a dream can be controlled before it occurs. To me, this technique is a simple thing, of which I'm only part of the equation.

This is how I do it: First, I ask God, the spirits at my side, and the angels at my four corners to either teach me about something I would like to know about or to answer a specific question that I have. Second, I go to sleep.

The spirits and angels that have gathered around me—as I explained in the last chapter—now participate in fabricating the dream I have requested.

I also reiterate that only God, the angels and those spirits whom I love or who love me are allowed to assemble or infiltrate my dreams. The last thing I need is some ornery spirit giving me misguided information just for the fun of it.

My work begins, though, when I awake the next morning or after the dream. I first try to remember what I have dreamt. I am usually successful, but sometimes my memory escapes me. After I've remembered my dream, I try to interpret it. That is, I try to interpret it so my human mind can understand it.

My success rate for the interpretation is not as high as my dream memory. It averages around 40 to 50 percent. When I am successful, I feel euphoric. When I fail, I don't dwell on it. I just let it go and say, "I will be able to remember and/or interpret the next dream."

I will now describe four of my successful dream applications, or programmed dreams. Remember that I work as a computer programmer by day? Well, a software "application" is the direct result of successful computer "programming." As I mentioned earlier, I believe that programming dreams can be just as straightforward, logical, and easy as programming a computer.

∼

In my affirmations, I mention that I want to receive divine wisdom. I also say I want this wisdom to infiltrate my mind and my spirit. The relevant affirmation is as follows:

> *"I want to receive divine wisdom today. I want this wisdom to infiltrate my mind and my spirit."*

One day, I was reading about spiritual growth, knowledge infusion, and mind expansion. This book, *Handbook of Metaphysics* by Tom Butler, wasn't pure pleasure reading, but it did spur some thought on my part.

What I read explained the necessity of expanding the mind and, consequently, the knowledge it contains. I started to question whether I was doing this to the greatest of my abilities. After a little thought, I concluded that I was expanding my mind, but the question remained: Was it adequate for my purposes?

That night, I decided to ask for divine help in finding an answer. All that I did was to ask the higher powers if I was expanding my mind adequately and, if so, how well I was doing it. I needed affirmation.

The answer came in my dream, as I hoped it would. In this particular dream, I was actually running, and I came upon an old man. He had gray hair and a long gray beard. (This seems to be my image of a wise man.)

What happened next is somewhat funny in retrospect, but it was also a very clear and straightforward answer. The wise man took a large pyramid-shaped crystal and turned it upside down. Next, he stuck the little pointy tip into the top of my head.

As I was not bothered by the weight of the large crystal, I continued to run around. It seemed to me that the large crystal pyramid was made out of clear quartz.

What this dream told me was that my mind was collecting knowledge. The inverted pyramid acted like a funnel to direct and concentrate information into my mind.

To me, a translucent crystal, a clear one in this case, filters what passes through it. For example, when light passes through a crystal, it is diffracted into a more pure light. So the fact that this pyramid was a clear crystal told me that I was filtering whatever information I gathered, in search of the most useful information. It's like when Jesus talked about separating the wheat from the chaff.

Before I had that dream, I had asked God and other divine powers to answer a question. I am confident that it was answered in my dream. And it was portrayed in an elegant way.

This is exactly what I mean by programming a dream. After I had that dream, I knew that I wanted to reaffirm on a daily basis what that dream had told me.

≈

My second dream application followed one of those lackluster days that are all too common. By lackluster, I mean that I just felt rather depressed, but not due to any specific event during that day. Maybe just the act of getting through the day brought me down.

Before I went to sleep that night, I asked God to make me feel better. I was not any more specific than that because I had no idea of what I needed. Fortunately, God heard me loud and clear and gave me a "dream" that to this day kindles pleasant memories.

I dreamed I was driving a car along a country road. It was a pretty drive with big trees along the road. I drove up a long curvy driveway that led to a big, beautiful house atop a hill.

I stepped out of the car and walked up to the house. A beautiful woman opened the door to greet me. We walked to the dining room, where a group was seated at a table. It seemed as if these people had been waiting for my arrival.

We ate a formal meal together. When we had finished, I walked to the front door. The woman who had greeted me walked with me. As I prepared to leave, we embraced and she said that she loved me and would see me later.

I woke up, my dream still racing through my mind, and looked at the clock. Only two and a half hours had passed since I had fallen asleep. I wanted to know who all the people in my dream were.

I felt wonderful. I was so excited that I did not go back to sleep for a few hours. That time was filled with a blissful peacefulness.

Although my earlier request had not been specific, I did program that dream. And it effectively gave me what I had needed.

≈

In the course of about three months, I had four recurring dreams. In each one, I found myself in a large house with four stories. Each time I found myself in the house, I walked up the stairs to the fourth floor. Once there, I walked into a bedroom.

The bedroom contained a queen-sized bed and beautiful wood furniture. The first thing I would do was walk over to a cedar chest.

I would then open the chest and start looking through the contents—a photo album, a wallet, and some jewelry. I felt like I was going through someone's possessions, but I could never figure out who they belonged to.

But even after four dreams of me up in that bedroom, I couldn't learn why I was there. So I became determined to discover why I kept going to that house.

This is where the dream programming part comes in.

A week after my fourth "house" dream, I awoke one morning at 5. I decided I wanted to go to the house of my earlier dreams.

I closed my eyes and asked Joy, my primary spirit guide, to take me back to the house I had seen repeatedly in earlier dreams. My intent to enlist Joy in helping me to solve the puzzle of why I kept dreaming about that house.

Thirty seconds later, I began to experience a sensation similar to the astral catalepsy I described in chapter 8.

I felt like my spirit was leaving my body. Again, I

heard a loud static or buzzing noise, as if my mind was vibrating. A few seconds later, I found myself back in that house. But this time, I knew that I was in control. I proceeded to walk up the four flights of stairs to the mysterious bedroom. This time, however, instead of going to the cedar chest, I went over to the window in the room. I looked out and saw a car approach. It stopped alongside the curb on the street directly in front of me.

A man stepped out of the car and approached the house. I felt a sense of urgency. Perhaps I sensed that the man was coming up to the bedroom.

I knew that Joy was there with me. I thought, "Now is the time to find out what this house means to me."

I said in a loud and stern voice, "Joy, tell me what this place means to me." Her reply was not what I expected.

She said, "I can't, you're blocking it."

Her words frustrated me. My first reaction was to make myself wake up and return to my body. Afterwards, I tried my best to put the whole situation out of my mind.

For the next couple of weeks, I did not even think about those house dreams. A part of me wanted to give up trying to figure out what that house meant to me.

My point here is that I made this final house dream happen, that is, if it really was a dream. And I was able to control it the way I wanted to, at least to a certain extent. Unfortunately, I could not control what my spirit guide said to me.

In order to bring a better cadence to this story, I finish it below. Although the end to my story is not about dream programming.

Around the same time as this last dream about the house, I had a past life regression (PLR) session scheduled. This is the same session I mentioned earlier. I remember that I was not sure if this regression thing would really work.

The person that was to guide my PLR session asked if there was anything I wanted to resolve during my regression. I told her about the house dreams.

During this session, I relaxed into a mild hypnotic state. My PLR guide asked me about the house. I had a mental picture of the house and saw myself sitting on a swing on the front porch. Somehow, I felt convinced that I had once lived in that house. Although I can't be sure I actually lived there, I never had another house dream after that, and I felt that I had reached enough of a resolution.

I don't think that these dreams were an indication of anything negative. And I'm satisfied with the outcome. If, in the future, I start having similar dreams again, then I might be concerned.

≈

In the first part of this book, I referred to a sea fishing trip my family and I went on. The destination was Vancouver Island, British Columbia, Canada. On the trip I met some wonderful people, but my relationship to one of those people turned out to be special.

His name was Sam Spring. The name he preferred, however, was Sam Eagle Feather. Sam was a full-blooded Apache Indian, 67 years old. He claimed to be the last Apache to have been born in a wikkiup, a type of portable house Native Americans once lived in, on a reservation in Arizona.

One afternoon I went to eat lunch with my family, and Sam accompanied us. On the way to the restaurant, Sam named my father Big Bear and me Little Bear. My father, my sister, and I have some Comanche and Cherokee ancestry. Sam knew this, which is why he gave us those names.

Sam died about three years later. But I didn't forget what he had called me.

About a year after he died, I went to sleep one night after asking Sam's spirit to come into my dream so we could visit. Later that night, I dreamed of playing with a little black bear. I had a lot of fun playing with that bear.

When I awoke, I realized that this had been Sam's way of visiting me. Even though he'd named *me* Little

Bear, his appearance in that dream as a bear was something that I could understand.

Because it is independent of the physical laws that govern earth, this dream programming technique will always remain one of my favorite ways to reach out and touch someone. That is, someone not in this world.

Dream programming is a supreme way to get information from our Ultimate Reality. But even more, dreams serve many wonders on a silver platter to all of us. All we have to do is make a sincere effort to listen and learn from these dreams and their wonders.

CHAPTER 18

$\sim$

Nighttime Prophecy

ALTHOUGH IT SEEMS I LEARN MORE each time I try dream programming, I think I have discovered its highest and best use. Dream programming seems especially valuable when it influences your life in a significant way, as it has for me. On the night this dream occurred, I was having one of my fits of uncertainty about my place here on earth and questioning my life's purpose. As I mentioned in chapter 1, I do believe that everything happens for a reason. And I try to go with the flow. The flow of life, that is. But sometimes I can't help but interrupt this flow.

My days usually consist of eight hours of work, two hours of driving time, and about four hours of personal time where I either compose music, read, or write, in addition to eating and occasionally having a workout at the gym. I sleep about ten hours a night. I've learned that less than ten hours makes it difficult to get through the next day.

But sometimes I stop and ask myself, "What am I doing?" These are times when I feel like I'm just going through the motions of life. To be honest, my ataxia often brings about these fits of uncertainty, but even before I had ataxia I periodically would get bored.

There are times when my job is stimulating, but for the most part it is routine. In the back of my mind, I know that I could be doing more with my life.

Recently, I used the dream programming technique to see if God would reveal my purpose in this life. The resulting dream only foretold one of my future efforts. However, I was pleased with the dream, because I had not known it was possible to learn the information I did. But, as I'll share with you, it is.

I dreamed I went on a trip to one of the towns where I spent a part of my childhood—Beaver, Oklahoma. It appeared somewhat different from what I remember.

The big difference was that there were a series of small commercial shops on a boardwalk. Although it was now a busy place with more people around, I felt reassured to be back.

I walked along the boardwalk and visited each shop.

At the end of the boardwalk was a school where I met a group of people.

As I walked into the school with the others, I saw a vast open area. I could not see any walls, but I felt it was an extremely large building. The peculiar thing was that this area was outdoors. I saw a large meadow with hills, grass, and trees. Scattered throughout the meadow were small groups of people engaged in various activities, such as track and field sports and animal training. I walked past one of those groups and saw that its members had many books. Each person was busy reading.

I looked at the titles of the books and saw that they were books about various religions, philosophies, and esoteric movements. Two titles I remember were *The Nag Hammadi Library* and *Alchemy*. As I've already mentioned, *TNHL* is a real book. But I don't know if *Alchemy* is a real title. I assumed that *Alchemy* was about the Renaissance-era alchemy movement.

I kept walking and eventually arrived at a table where a dozen or so people were seated. I remained standing, however. I immediately felt that there was a connection between those people at the table and those in the scattered groups. The people at the table seemed to be governing the assembled groups. Representatives from each group were lined up to seek advice (I felt) from those seated at the table.

I lined up with the others. When it was my turn to approach the table, I walked up to one of the men.

I told him, "I think I should join the group with the books." I was eager to read those books.

He said, "Through all of your work with the handicapped, you are now ready to be transferred into the group with the books." In this dream, I was in one of the groups of people in the meadow, and we worked helping people with disabilities.

I walked over to my work group. This was the group from which I was now graduating. I told each member of the group, one by one, that I was leaving them and my work with people with disabilities to go to the group with all the books. I said goodbye to everyone.

∾

This dream seemed to be a clue from God about my direction in life and accurately described my process of spiritual growth. At the time of this dream, I was ready to learn more, and books have always been a significant part of learning.

In the months prior to this dream, I had attempted to write a "spiritual" book, but I had soon lost interest and stopped writing. Then, two weeks after I had decided to work on the book again, I had this dream.

I gained more insight as I continued to analyze the

dream. Maybe the sight of those books symbolized my own writing efforts. Perhaps it was telling me that writing one—or more—books is among the most important endeavors I can undertake.

What was said to me was also something I picked up on. Maybe the man at the table's use of the word "handicap" referred to my own physical limitations. When he said, "Through all of your work," he may have been alluding to my efforts to cope with my own ataxia. Because it is work!

I believe that my experiences since I've had ataxia have brought me to a place where I know I have important information to convey. And one of the best ways I can do this is through writing.

◈

CHAPTER 19

Everyday Blessings and Divine Intervention

I DON'T KNOW WHAT IT IS about fast food restaurants, but a couple of well-known chains have made it into this book, in the form of two simple and common stories that illustrate divine intervention and everyday blessings. A few years back, I drove a friend home after a day of work. On the way, we decided to stop at a McDonald's fast food restaurant and get something to eat.

I remember going into the bathroom at the restaurant and looking into the mirror. I thought, "My hair is getting long—I need to get it cut." Back at the table, I told my friend, "I really need a haircut, but I don't have a barber" (meaning a barber I knew and trusted). I wondered where to find a place that would do a good job of cutting my hair. I had found from experience that going to one of those *Haircuts for Less* places was a gamble. After a "hair stylist" at one such place cut my ear, I had a reason to dislike and avoid cheap haircut places.

Amber was in town that weekend. Later that night, she and I went over to visit another friend.

After a few minutes of conversation, my friend's wife offered to cut my hair. Although I had not previously mentioned my hair dilemma, it turned out that she was a professional beautician. A few hours earlier, I had no idea where I could get my hair cut. And now I had been given a solution. I silently thanked my spirit guides for helping me solve my problem. I know my spirit guides to attend to my problems around the clock, "24/7."

≈

At my office, I have a window in my cubicle. I can see a Good Times fast food restaurant across a busy street—a typical urban-blight sort of view, perhaps, but better than a brick wall.

One morning as I was looking out of my window, I saw one of the restaurant's employees out picking up trash in the parking lot. I thought, "That woman works very hard. It's not fun to work that hard and get paid so little." I've experienced such work.

I said to myself, "I bless you," and asked God to bless her also.

The next day, I went out for lunch. I did not feel like eating a "sit down" lunch in a restaurant, so I went through the drive-through at Good Times instead. Because of my physical condition, I drive just to get across the street—it's a dangerous street to cross on foot, anyhow.

At the drive-through window, I was served by the same woman I had seen in the parking lot the morning before. She said, "How are you? It's so good to see you. How have you been?" I had been served by her before, but this was the first time she had said anything more than the usual "Come again."

~

And that's how divine intervention and everyday blessings work. A few more stories here illustrate the wonders of Mother and Father God and of our spirits.

~

Toward the end of my time working in downtown Denver, I worked in a high-rise office building. I had to take the elevator to get to my office. Stairs and I do not get along. And the elevator ride took only about 30 seconds, providing it made no stops.

One Monday morning, I stepped on the elevator, and as usual was joined by a few other workers. One lady decided to tell everyone in the car how she had thrown her back out over the weekend. She complained that she was going to have a bad week because of all the pain. I said, "Don't worry; you will be back to normal soon."

As she walked off the elevator she turned back toward me and said, "Thank you."

Throughout life, I always try to say something uplifting when faced with another's negativity or pain. I never really know how helpful my words may be, but they come directly from my spirit.

Comforting words are special, because they seem to emanate from our higher selves. Such words are one of the best things in life.

≈

In the dead of the Colorado winter, I bought a small rosebush. It was in the floral department of the local grocery store and had blossomed into many beautiful little red flowers. I just had to buy it. As I do with any plant I buy, I asked for Mother and Father God to bless the rosebush's delicate life.

In the beginning of December, it looked great. It stayed inside and I watered it a lot.

By the beginning of April, however, the rosebush had no flowers left and was struggling to survive. The main reason was that the handful of soil in its planter had been depleted of nutrients.

The rosebush was beginning to die. I kept it going with lots of water for the next two weeks. In the middle of April, I set it out on the front porch. This was my way of reminding myself to plant it in the flower bed in the outside garden.

Instead, the rosebush sat there for two more weeks. Every time I saw it, I remembered that I needed to plant it. This happened more than a few times. It continued its struggle for survival. But after two weeks, it looked dead.

Now I felt bad. Guilt overcame me because I knew I could have helped it earlier. I went and bought some topsoil so I could plant it in the flower bed right away. Doing this made me feel better, but I figured my efforts were too little too late.

For the next week or so, the rosebush appeared not to change noticeably. I was sure it was dead. But, during that time, I prayed daily for it to live.

About two weeks later, it began to show signs of life. I believe that my prayers were a significant factor in its recovery. Maybe I gave that rosebush a reason to live.

Today, it's over 10 inches tall and looks healthy. I hope that it will bloom within the next year.

∾

While writing this book, I went to the doctor to have my annual physical. Part of the standard procedure included a blood test. I did not expect any bad results from this test.

A few days later, my doctor's office called me at work. My "bad" cholesterol was 251, as opposed to the norm of 200 or less. My doctor said that this number wasn't that terrible but was concerned that it might get worse.

At his request, I went back to see him, and he told me that he was giving me two months to lower it. If I didn't, I would have to start taking cholesterol-lowering medication.

I came out of his office determined to lower the number without having to make major alterations in my diet. My dietary changes were indeed insignificant. I drank about half as many glasses of milk as usual. But that was about it. I continued to eat steak and lobster tail once a week.

I did do two things, though. First, I worked out at my gym three times a week instead of less frequently, as I had been doing. Second, I asked God for help. I said, "God, ataxia is about all I can handle health-wise, so take away this stupid cholesterol thing."

Eight weeks later, my cholesterol was 50 points lower. My doctor said that I was fine. Immediately after this news, I silently thanked God for the help. Hopefully, if I keep exercising and praying, my cholesterol won't get out of hand in the future.

～

A few months before I began work on this book, I purchased a set of cards with angel pictures on them. What caught my eye initially was the beautiful artwork.

The cards are not like those in a standard playing card deck. According to the box they came in, they are "Oracle Cards." Ever since our Mother God asked me to tell her, "What is in the cards?" (chapter 14), I've seen cards like this in a different light.

The cards are supposed to present accurate divination messages from angels when used in various "spreads"; that is, laying out and arranging the cards in a certain way.

One morning as I prepared for work, I saw those cards as I grabbed my watch. I thought, "I should try using them and just see what happens." Right then, I asked God a question and for the answer to manifest in the appropriate card.

My question was, "Will my ataxia situation ever leave me while I'm in this life?" I qualified it with "In this life," because I strongly believe that when I return to a spiritual essence, I won't be burdened by a physical body and all the limitations imposed by it.

After scrutinizing the cards for about 10 seconds, I selected one. I turned it over and saw a particularly pretty, angelic picture.

This card read, "Keep charging ahead, for a miraculous solution awaits you." I knew something special had just happened. I thought, "Maybe these cards do work." Those words helped strengthen my hope that my ataxia will leave me.

But don't get me wrong. I'm not expecting God to just magically abolish my ataxia and whatever its root cause is. I do believe, however, it will eventually leave me. I know it might be a lengthy and difficult process, but I will continue to work toward it.

∽

CHAPTER 20

Meditation Destination

I WAS SO HAPPY TO COME UP with a rhyming title that I gave this chapter an extra effort. In this chapter, I describe how I participate in meditation, a truly divine pastime.

In late 1999, I learned about meditation. Soon after that, I began to meditate—or, at least to try to. Even since that time, meditation has not been my strong point. Sure, I think it is a great technique, but I don't devote enough time to it. Many people say that you have to practice to get good at it. I believe them.

But I have constructed, in my mind, my own meditation places. Just the visualization of these places seems to satisfy the reason why I meditate in the first place.

You are always welcome to visit my meditation places.

Who knows, we might share a laugh if we're both there at the same time!

❧

I've mentioned my vacation to British Columbia, Canada. It was so beautiful there that I felt compelled to make it a permanent part of my life. For me, it is one of those special places.

As I said previously, we visited the strait on the east side of Vancouver Island. There, the water is filled with islands. These islands are like little forested ecosystems of their own. We were based at Campbell River, where our friend Sam lived. One day we headed southeast in our boat, hoping for some great salmon fishing.

About an hour later, we came upon a small island. It was only about two hundred feet in diameter. The island itself was lovely, full of pine, cedar, and fir trees. Slowly, we passed the island and continued to look for a good fishing spot.

❧

A couple of months after I had returned home from that trip, I began to learn about meditation. But some of the meditation techniques I was reading about seemed to lack a personal touch. I believe that a meditation works best when it is custom-tailored for the person using it.

I decided to formulate my own meditation place. I remembered that little island right off of Vancouver Island, and thought that it would work nicely.

Now I envision a two-story house on that island. The house itself covers most of the island. The first time I used this meditation, I mentally designed the outside and inside and furnished the interior. Each time I use this meditation, my intangible house always appears the same.

My house is white on the outside and the entry is on the north. The outside of the house is decorated in American Colonial style.

The interior is completely finished. The walls are painted white and the carpet is white. All of the furniture is made either of walnut, cherry, or mahogany wood.

The most remarkable piece of furniture is a piano. It is dark and is finished with oil. Each time I go to the house, there is a pianist playing Romantic music, like that composed by Chopin and Brahms.

Now for the reason why I go there. . .

In the front room is a plush couch without a back. When I enter the house, I move toward that comfortable couch.

I lie down and relax. There are usually one to 10 people and/or angels in the immediate vicinity. These people and angels are healers. They heal me simply by laying their hands on me.

This meditation is always calming and relaxing. And, best of all, I don't have to sit in a car for 30-plus hours to get to British Columbia.

Now if I could just take my physical body there and get it healed. . .

≈

The last day we were on the ocean, we took our boat north through an area known as the Narrows. The people that lived on Vancouver Island told us that boating through this waterway is dangerous because of strong currents resulting from the tides. Successful navigation through the Narrows is dependent upon knowledge of the tides.

The sky was overcast. Ever since I can remember, I've always enjoyed an overcast sky. It's like I can feel the electricity in the air. On this day, it added an aura of mystique to our adventure through the Narrows.

A few months after I returned from our Canadian fishing trip, I designed one other meditation. So from that same trip, I fabricated two meditations, one inspired from the small island as I described above and one inspired by the Narrows.

Like the meditation place from above, this one is on an island about 30 miles north of the island in my previous meditation.

My meditation usually begins with me somewhere in those Narrows. I never swim or travel by boat. I always walk or run on the water. After I travel a mile or so, I approach an island.

This island is about eight acres in size. It is filled with trees and green grass. The eastern side of the island reveals a path leading to a magnificent structure reminiscent of a large gothic castle. This castle is entirely made of white marble.

I have yet to explore this castle completely. I always enter a large hallway and then turn to the left through the double doors to a small parlor.

The parlor is decorated with highly polished white marble on the floors and the walls. There is a fireplace with a beautiful mantel in the center of the room. Placed around the fireplace are a few marble chairs. The chairs have cushions on them in order to make them comfortable. If there'd been no cushions, I might have had to boycott that castle!

When I visit this castle, I always end up sitting in one of those chairs. Before I even enter the parlor area, there are usually one or more people seated there.

I usually come prepared with a question or two. My

questions are always answered by those seated around me. But my problem lies with interpreting or understanding the answers later when I end the meditation.

Every time I use this meditation, I sit with a different group of people than those I sat with before. Sometimes I don't recognize anyone, but maybe my spirit knows these people from past times.

As of now, it is still difficult for me to learn anything that I can use in my life from this meditation. I'm going to keep trying, though. One day I might have a breakthrough.

∼

CHAPTER 21

This, That, and the Other

I THOUGHT THAT I HAD COMPLETED the content of this book, when I went back to my early notes and found a couple of experiences that I had meant to include. Here is one:

I awoke one morning at 5 and thought, "I want something really awesome to happen. Something I have never experienced before." I knew that someone out there had to hear my plea. So I just closed my eyes and waited.

A couple of minutes later, something began to happen. I felt the vibrations and heard the familiar buzzing noise of astral catalepsy. I started to go out of my body.

I remember thinking, "I wish this transition would hurry up and finish." I sometimes get bored easily. I was eager for that which awaited me.

I was in my room. I saw my body sleeping. Next, a very beautiful and exotic-looking woman appeared, about five feet away. Slowly, she walked toward me. Although I wondered what her intentions were, I was not afraid.

When she stood only inches from me, she put her arms around me and said, "I love you and I'm always with you." I said, "I love you, too," and embraced her.

After this hug, I returned to my body. I awoke and thought, "Could she have been my soul mate?"

I do believe in soul mates. But I also believe both entities almost never incarnate on earth at the same time. So it makes sense to me that my soul mate would probably exist in Ultimate Reality.

Things are looking bright in the future.

∾

For the Christmas of 2003, my mother, my father and I stayed with Amber and her husband at their house in Grand Junction, Colorado.

As I went to sleep on Christmas Eve, I asked Joy to let me experience the Christmas celebration on the Other Side. To make my request more specific, I added that I wanted to experience the celebration that was in the same geographic area as Amber's house; in other words, the mirror location of that spot where their house was in Grand Junction. It is my belief that every location on this earth is duplicated in Ultimate Reality and they share a location relative to each other. For example, the North Pole is at the same location in Ultimate Reality as it is on earth.

I didn't think my spirit was up to traveling anywhere. The drive was enough traveling for me that day!

At about 2 AM, I left my body briefly. I heard lots of laughing and music playing. It was a party. I did not really "see" anything. Not with my eyes, that is. But much of the laughter seemed close by.

While I was out, I thanked Joy for fulfilling my request.

~

One night after work, I sat down to watch the game show *Wheel of Fortune* with my father. For no particular reason, I closed my eyes and started singing "Somewhere over the Rainbow" to myself. I thought, "What a beautiful song."

I opened my eyes and looked at the TV. The puzzle was "Lions, Tigers and Bears." The completion of the clue they gave was "Oh my."

That puzzle represented a well-known quote from the *Wizard of Oz*, the movie that also gave us the song

"Somewhere over the Rainbow." To me, that is one of the best songs ever written.

This was not *déja vu*, but it was something like that. Maybe I will eventually learn what this experience is called. Other than coincidence.

I do believe in coincidences. But I am convinced this was not one. My belief is that with a plethora of variables in the environment, the necessary synchronizations to make a coincidence are few and far between.

~

The final part of this chapter is not an experience. It's just me giving credit to God where credit is due.

Throughout this book, I have referred to my affirmations. This book, and my life, for that matter, is a testament to the powerful benefits of adopting and practicing a set of affirmations.

Affirmations are a type of prayer. To me, they're just custom-tailored prayers. It's great to say a prayer like the Lord's Prayer often, but I think affirmations can be even more liberating and satisfying.

I guess what I'm trying to say is this: For me, a regimen of affirmations enables me to align myself with God. That is, to align my will with God's will. And in truth, I want to align myself with God as much as I possibly can while I'm in this life.

I recommend to everyone that if you want a close relationship or alignment with Mother or Father God, Jesus, Muhammad, the universal life force, or whatever you want to call it, then start using, on a regular basis, a set of personalized affirmations.

Afterword

~

I THANK YOU for reading this book. And I hope that my soul path touches you in a meaningful way.

Writing this book was important and therapeutic. I have complained more than once about my physical condition. "Complaining" like this has helped me share my burden.

Recently, I had a short conversation with someone I had worked with briefly. As we met in passing, he asked me how I was. I replied, "I'm doing great. How are you?" He said, "I'm doing fine. I'm just happy to be alive."

I had never heard anyone say this before. "I'm just happy to be alive." I thought, "Yes, it really is a blessing just to be alive."

Now that I walk slowly, I take the time to admire my surroundings. I do this even if I'm just walking from my house to my car. Day or night, I take the time to appreciate what is around me.

Also, since my ataxia has manifested, I've learned to

appreciate people. I know how wonderful it is to return a smile to a stranger. I've discovered a good feeling I get just from holding a door open for someone.

My purpose in writing this book was to glorify life. The life that is mine, yours and, ultimately, ours. To glorify life is to glorify that which we are all a part of. And to me, that ultimate power is God and the Christ Consciousness that dwells within each and every one of us.

Yes, I am happy to be alive. And I hope that we all are, or can learn to be, happy to be alive.

∼

Affirmations

~

"Mother and Father God, today I live for you. You are the commander of my ship. I am a soldier of your faith. I will always love you. Please guide me today.

God, help me to be a strong and ever-increasing light in this world. Help me to love and care for everyone I encounter today.

God, surround me with the white light of the Holy Spirit. Also surround me with a spiritually loving and healing light. Let everyone that enters into my presence today benefit from this light.

Let my higher self rise to the place where it should be today. I want to function from there. Also, help me to prevent my lower self from unduly influencing me.

I want to receive divine wisdom today. I want this wisdom to infiltrate my mind and my spirit.

Today, I want the left and right sides, hemispheres, of my mind to come together in equilibrium and perfect harmony. Help me to achieve a balance between my intellectual center (left side) and my emotional center (right side).

Joy, Marcel, and Marilyn, my spirit guides, guide me through this day. Assist me in my decisions and help me through any negative experiences. Help me to make today the best day I can make it.

I ask for the love and protection of the angels to be with me today.

Jesus, walk with me today. Help me to have great physical balance. Help me to walk like I know I can. Protect me from falling and, possibly, hurting myself.

God, I want to have a great day and to do the best I can."

I would love to hear from you with thoughts on this book or anything else. I can be contacted at:

Brandon Campbell
Ascending Realm Publishing
PO Box 2223, Centennial, Colorado
USA 80161-2223

Email: brandon@ascendingrealm.com
Website: www.ascendingrealm.com